Night Travelers

Night Travelers

Poems by

Carol Rucks

Cover design by Shay Culligan
Cover photo by Mark McHugh
Author photo by Mark McHugh

ISBN: 978-1-63980-668-3
Library of Congress Control Number: 2024950128

Kelsay Books
502 South 1040 East, A-119
American Fork, Utah 84003
Kelsaybooks.com

To Mark, Nick, Angela, and David

Acknowledgments

The author wishes to thank the editors of the following publications for printing these poems, some forthcoming, others appearing in slightly different versions:

ArtLife: "Child Labor"
Blue Unicorn: "Night Travelers"
Chronicle Alternative: "December"
Earth's Daughters: "In the Bardo," "What the Dead Remember," "The Transfer"
Full Circle: "Crows"
Little by Little the Bird Builds Its Nest: A Bird Anthology, Paris Morning Publications: "Crows," "Robin," "The Song of the Common Sparrow"
Northfield Magazine: "The Wild Dogs of Mexico"
The Orchards Poetry Journal: "The Yellow Glow"
Portage: "September Evening with an Old Album"
Redheaded Stepchild Online: "A Dream of Barbados"
Southwest Journal: "I've Come to Observe"
Whistling Shade: "Robin," "This Kind of Humble Day," "Edinburgh"

Thanks also to Karen Kelsay, publisher, and to Shay Culligan, book designer, and to the many others who had a hand in shaping this book, including June Blumenson, Kate Green, Sandra Sidman Larson, Mary Junge, Shannon King, Roseann Lloyd, Cynthia Fuller, and Mark McHugh.

Contents

III

The moon is itself and is lost among the stars
—Joan Murray

All maps are misleading
—Paul Theroux

Memory's nobody's fool,
and keeps close to the ground
—Charles Wright

I

The Yellow Glow

The pale gleam
inside houses at night
sparks a fierce curiosity.
It calls to me
as I walk along this empty
street, wandering a little
off path and into a strange
neighborhood.
A slight breeze
kicks up as I pause
in the muddy dark,
waiting for something
to happen, half-expecting
someone
to open a side door,
invite me in.
I should know
better, but the yellow
glow draws on me
insect to flower
with its steady flame,
pulling me
to the heat and fire
of other lives.

In a Dream Someone Calls

on an old black telephone, rotary dial,
reaching in from another century.
A small voice, neither masculine
nor feminine, squeaky and weak,
has important questions.
And you wonder how the dead reach
out after hours, late at night
when everyone sleeps.
He asks in a whisper
if I really loved him
when the trees shivered with new
leaves and our bodies sparkled
like fireflies. And did anyone
remember the tulips
opening brilliant red
with pale interiors.
And did the April grass
scented with sun
still glisten under our feet
while little clouds floated by.

White Corolla

It came from my father-in-law
when he went into assisted living.
At first, I didn't like it,
it smelled mildly of old professor,
and the brakes were soft, the steering mush.

We cleaned it up and drove it all over town,
to the beach, to the movies,
to the wharf restaurants at White Bear Lake.

No one would ever steal this car,
twenty years old, chipped white paint
on the sides, a CD player that never worked.

In a dream I drove it to a church parking lot,
left it there, and walked away.

But we actually traded it in.
Traded in part of the family,
gave away the white ghost that held
the scent of my second father
on the dashboard and in the glove compartment.

We traded it in the way a divorcing woman
exchanges the near failures for the half-known
promises. How it hurts
to see it there in the lot at Maplewood Toyota,
a small agony. We let it go
for something shiny and blue.

After the Night of Straight Line Winds

I'd like to see something beautiful
not corrupted by the rain and chaos of a thunderhead,
or the terrible flight of a tossed tree
landing on a center beam, garage roof smashed.
Another tree lies broken, second house down.
A third across the alley, a silver maple,
flopped up whole on the ground
like a great dying fish.
The light surprises us, too much sun
for plants that need shade.
Sticks and leaves, debris of electrical workers,
and odd bits of circular metal are scattered everywhere.
I'd like to see something serene and calm,
landscapes by Cezanne or Matisse,
or just my garden, the way it bloomed
and fluttered when I stood here
the day before yesterday.

Sometimes the Green Light

shines all the way in, and the darkness
drifts away, moves
outward to the lining of a cloud.
A maple, a Norway pine, a catalpa,
the three of them linger in a green glow
against a sea of green, some high up,
some low to the ground.
All of my windows are open
to the shiver of the daily grass,
flicker of cottonwood leaves.
Yellow sun and blue sky
create this green, this quiver
and turn of chlorophyll,
green plus heat, green plus water,
sparks the crusted seed
waiting inside.

Water Snake

In the pond a gray snake
with diamond markings
wove through high water.
I kept back and edged
toward the pebbly shore.
No one said this could happen
this far north,
while the sun whispered
away stubborn clouds.
Somehow I knew
that surprises bring danger:
wind with sleet,
rock with river bottom.
The snake undulated thru weeds
the way geese muscle air,
winding a path to
darker wilds.

Encounter

No doorbell but a solid pounding
on the maple back door

a boy with a Roman fringe over his eyes
peered through the dusty panel

perhaps seeking cash or weed
with those liquid caramel eyes

his trembling right hand on the knob
had me reaching for the yellow broom

I use for chasing squirrels and rabbits
out of my husband's patch of kale

but after his five-second seduction
he stared down my mismatched pajamas

and smirked broadly to himself
as if he were my own wayward son

The Bees

I wandered my garden today
to check on cone flowers and dianthus,
scraping the dark soil for moisture.

Stepping in
with my head down, wasps
spun in the air, a pale butterfly
flicked the generous light.

What I saw next delighted me:
two bumble bees having sex
on a burnt spike of bee balm.

The marriage of fat and thrust
gleamed with bulging eyes,
ignoring me
as if I were a stranger.

The Visitor from Cleveland

arrives an hour early, without explanation.
She brings in her gifts:
a giant chocolate bar, a bag of Brussels sprouts.
She means well, but the lack of wine
will slow down the weekend.

She hangs her coat over a chair,
the way a man does when he wants a second date.

The visitor will surprise everyone
with her colorful T-shirts
that somehow match her many lipsticks.

There will be movies to see,
clubs to stretch out in, parties to crash.

Arguments are bound to begin over politics,
with really enjoyable hair-splitting.
She knows how to pontificate
after just one episode of *Meet The Press*.

And later, she will crank up
Sonic Youth on her phone.
And everyone will flounce and dance,
shaking the floor boards of the little house
that just can't hold her.

Walking Through the Reformation

Here in the throng at the Minneapolis Institute of Art,
we slog like drugged cattle
through the art exhibit on Martin Luther.
His life and struggles are set before us
in heavy bibles, miniature hymnals,
handmade furniture.
We push ourselves forward
to see the oddities: the peaked cap of a plague doctor,
the scatological etchings, instructions for the faithful
painted on rough wooden altars.
We inch north and look,
hold still, everyone in winter sweaters, dull
coats, stunned in our sackcloths of curiosity.
We keep the line orderly, shuffle
ahead, cheek by jowl,
sneak a last glimpse of the Catholic gold,
the scarlet robes behind us, the beauty
we sometimes need, pretending to touch and inhale
the scandal of crimson and silver,
before it's all made
plain.

Appetites

I tried to hold on to love,
friendship, a good job.
The more I squeezed what I had
the more the juice and sugar dribbled out.
I tried to learn by exploration, uncovering
big cities, foreign countries, dark mountains.
The further I stepped out
in my new boots, the more exhausted I became.
Finally, I slowed down a little, understood
a friend gradually, stayed in one place
for awhile, fell in love
with a city park, a small tavern,
the back of a man's head.
I broke it down into edible parts,
instead of gobbling up the world
like Rossini at his feasting table
humming a Spanish melody,
while eating roast duck, asparagus
fried in butter, sardines in wine sauce,
wolfing everything down
and savoring nothing.

The Transfer

I was fascinated
by the dark elegance
coming out of his mouth.
He moved easily
between lovers and strangers.
The sidewalk seemed to roll
up to him.
He stayed up late, drank
good wine. I wanted to steal
some part of him, let
myself become night.

To catch up
I waited in the gritty tangle
of Wisconsin Avenue
for the number thirty bus.
I saw its square shadow
tremble behind the body
of a truck, yellow roof lights
glaring in a row.
It inched forward
as I fingered the smooth skin
of a transfer in my hand.
Loose paper and dirt
rolled over my shoes.

A cold wind unbuttoned
my coat and filled
the emptiness of my pockets
with a kind of sadness.
The street light near me
went blind.

And suddenly, my desire
crumbled in a black
frenzy of smoke.

Red Riding Hood

When the wolf leaned
in close, sniffed my scent,
I knew I had to run away
through forest and glen
to Grandmother's tidy house.
It didn't matter that my heels were high,
or that the wind opened my blouse.
I had my cell phone, a bit of cash,
and knew how to yell out loud.
Trouble was, I loved the wolf,
admired the glint and swagger,
the knives in his eyes.
I loved him at the well
when he spoke to me, water
like a river in his dark voice.
I loved him at the wood shed,
his hands and chest adoring me.
It took me years to batten down
the dusk, make a run for it
through the green-dark woods,
find a clearing full of sky
to throw my shoes away.

The Common Dreams

You're out at a dinner party
at a friend's new house
and forget to wear any shoes,
and perhaps only a towel is wrapped
around your naked torso.
Or you're in high school
once again, armful of books,
though you're in your sixties
wearing only pink underwear
in the green hallway.
And you can't find your locker
or the notes you need for the final test
of the last algebra class you'll ever need.
But luck can change quickly,
and the locker appears
behind an old boyfriend
dressed in a paisley shirt,
and just in time it opens
like the spirited finale
of a Netflix rom-com.

Door to Door

Fruit-eating hominids
came to the front door yesterday,
giving away copies of Darwin's *Origin of Species*.
They stood under the trees
looking plump and well-fed in their brown suits.
One grabbed an apple
from a nearby tree, tossed it
silently to the other.
I accepted a copy of the book,
and turned them out to the empty street.
Silver maples and burr oaks fluttered
and shook as they padded away.

If the Shoe Fits

wear it around the house
like a witch from the middle ages,
slouch toward the light of the moon.
Or, if you're out and about
in the wicked city, wear boots so black
everyone will know how much you love
dirty blues and rock and roll.
Do something crazy with your hair,
even if it heats up the collars
of some of your relatives
in the same way they steam up
at the barking of the neighbor's dog.
Don't be afraid to be yourself,
or to test out different selves
in your suburb or small town.
It may feel like it, but seriously,
no one is taking notes.

Phantom Doorbell

An anonymous letter came in the mail yesterday,
handwritten, in a style I didn't recognize.
It ripped me down, along with my husband,
our humor, our work history.
The woman who wrote it had a hard time
spelling all the words correctly.

Still, I felt the sting, and a loss
of dignity.

In the letter she claimed I didn't tip
enough at dinner, and that my husband lost
his Irish temper too easily.

And then the doorbell rang,
not once but twice, urgency in the chime,
but no one was there.

Why did this letter come to me, unsigned
and in a ragged scrawl, ghost-like,
full of venom and jealousy?
Was she an old friend I turned away,
a gaping difference between us?

The doorbell rang again,
perhaps there was an electrical short,
a dampness or rust
eating away at the insides, the wiring
unraveled, the connection undone.

She Always Dressed Up in Style

and wore the best that Goodwill had to offer.
Her hair looked sleek, day after day,
no matter the heat or humidity.
What came out of her mouth was sweet,
but tinged with the shine of youthful pride.
And sometimes her nose tilted up
with just a whiff of over-confidence.
She loved to go out to dinner,
discover new restaurants in the meandering
streets and byways of the city,
or to be engulfed by a noisy crowd
in an art museum, slide from painting
to painting, coffee in hand.
Sometimes, she's a mere blur
in front of me, a flash of warm light.
But, I shouldn't have let her in my kitchen
without explaining the rules
of house-keeping and friendship,
or let her burn our midnight snack
of toast and a mushroom omelet.
I still want her to be my companion,
after she takes my introductory course
on slowing down. I'll give her the chance
she gave me. I still love her.

The Preview

It happens at midnight
in January
during a sudden chill,
the sky turns black,
and animals scuttle
to hide beneath the porch.
From inside the house
a great silence enfolds us
like a series of veils
falling over faces
and doorways.
The walls darken
and the ceiling closes in
toward blackness.
But don't close
your eyes just yet.
Watch the night descend
over the dresser
and onto the bed.
Let it cover you slowly
before the trees disappear.
Listen to the confession
coming out of the mirror.
The voided windows
glisten with sleep
as a stillness takes over.

Night Travelers

Animals walk around
in the dark, ones we cannot see
or sniff out from our beds.
They are on the move
right now, some stronger
than a man.
They steal from room
to room, with great strength.
I think no one hears them
but me. No one speaks
about their hidden danger,
the fire in their breath.
Creaking interrupts the night
with whispers of curiosity and wonder,
in the attic and on the floor.
I can't name them
any longer, or stroke
their backs with my hands;
nor can I stop them
from going home.

False Memory of Purgatory

As the wind kicks up
in my darkest sleep, and the moon
sings to the birds of night,
I sometimes fall into a blinded trance
that is neither dream nor rest,
but a kind of tumbling downward.
There, I sense the ancients
wandering the darkened abyss
where Dante traveled with negligent souls
toward a ledge of obsidian.
I slip into the blackness for a minute
almost seeing the ones I knew,
but because of fear, because of
breath, I quickly return.

Driving Dream

I drove my new car
though my eyes wouldn't open.

I couldn't get them to budge
but I knew I was in Northeast Minneapolis

heading to the Credit Union to cash a check.
I could hear light traffic bumping along,

heading north over the potholes of Stinson Avenue,
but my eyes seemed to be glued shut.

I was too stubborn to pull over,
having traveled this far, sailing along

as if pulled by an invisible rope, the way love
or friendship moves us forward

though we think danger is just up ahead,
and good reasons exist

to give up, or at least slow down,
but we're not sure if anyone can help.

I could hear footsteps
running alongside the car

as the voice of a stranger
called out with meaningful instructions.

In the Bardo

You left dirty footprints on the threshold
between this world and the next.
Your darkness shimmered in the pale exit.
But that was last year's sorrow,
now ice melts into an earthly mud.
I can't carry the grit on my skin anymore,
toil on it like old homework.
I'll watch you float through indifferent
corridors, trolling for lost light.
I'll listen at the window
for discordant melodies.

Garden Cycle

I've smelled this air before,
inhaled the rotting cabbage,
compost of melon rind and banana
humus ripening in the sun.

And now I taste it in the back of my throat
as I leave the garden, the wind catches
in the cavern of my mouth.

It is a common thing to lose
nest, warmth, breath.
To graduate from child to rock,
careless love to dirt.

The acrid fume holds
when I see the little bones,
tender bird in the grass.

At the Zoo

Mid-September at the Como Zoo,
the one remaining Greater Kudo and I
have a staring contest.
I worry about the flies twitching
his back, and the cruel sun
setting his tail on fire.
The end of summer can get the best of us,
as we search for companions
in our small plots of garden
and patches of grass.
Along this wooden fence, skeletons
of green thorn bushes cast
a daring shadow.
The Greater Kudo and I
have the whole lonely sky to ourselves.

The Warm Scent of the Sun

dissipates in winter.
Trees go to sleep standing up
the way horses do, going stiff
and quiet. Rabbits gather,
huddling in piles of odorless leaves
under stoops and wooden decks.
The snow itself has a low-key life,
moving in like a tide without a fragrance
over the slumbering grass.
When shards of yellow ice fall
from roofs, they send out no aroma,
but I can smell laundry being over-done
next door, a shaft of hot air
blows clouds of detergent on our house.
And someone nearby leans off
their back porch with a lit cigarette,
barely dressed in a sweater and yoga pants.
Despite the knives in the wind, it's worth
getting out to sniff the crested drifts
that try to hide the perfumes
of other seasons.

Lazy February

For two days I called in sick.
At home, I did nothing.
I stopped sweeping the kitchen,
allowed the back steps to become fuzz.
The gray shapes of rabbits
grew under our bed.
I should have told you
I let the mop sleep in,
gave the broom the week off.
In the long hours since,
I saw a red-tailed hawk chase
a small bird into oblivion.
Squirrels tumbled and teased
up a staircase of bark.
Various colors lit up the sky:
tangerine clouds, golden snow, silver roofs.
I excused myself at the windowsill
to watch Pre-Cambrian swirls
of stems and ferns
harden into panel friezes.

North of Clear Lake

We followed three hipsters
dressed in black
down the grassy path
to the spot where Buddy Holly
and his friends
crashed in a farm field.
The barren skies of Iowa
seemed to be moaning little
songs of comfort for us.
I swear I heard music,
but it was only the wind turbines
in a neighboring field,
a lament churning like an opera
by Philip Glass.
Soybeans in the field
looked fresh and young,
too healthy to be sacrificed
by our heavy boots.
The melody continued
above us, unwound,
lifted, and turned.

Of All the Fools

to pick as a friend
I picked the shiniest one,
the one with perfect hair and teeth
who knew her way around the bar stool
and the classroom.
Now that she's moved out of state
we don't call or text
or tackle whatever platform is left
to our advantage,
keeping loneliness close.
Still, there seems to be a trembling
late at night, from her dream
to mine, a whisper of regret
floats across the country
like an uncoiling fog
where the sleepless
and unsure drift and unwind,
mist to mist,
sorrow to sorrow.

Sometimes an Ex-Friend Shows Up

in a black and white dream
while you're minding your own business
standing under a tree in your pajamas.
And there she is in her tall glory,
combed hair, perfectly fitting jeans,
someone you were once close to
before a common betrayal.
You give her a hug, because in dreams
we don't know any better.
The chitchat starts and won't stop
and before you know it,
the two of you have decided to go
into therapy together, as if solutions
really existed between the fully broken-hearted.
And later, you find yourself complimenting
her new haircut, all the while knowing
that too much water has already gone
under the bridge from a great reverberating
and churning river.

Once at a Party

when it was very late, the husband
slipped into a well-lit kitchen
following a young woman,
very blonde, a cleft chin,
and suddenly everyone understood
they'd fallen in love with each other.
It's the kind of romance that lasts
exactly three hours, but is nonetheless
a pure thing, made up clean and fresh
from small talk, Sangria, and popcorn.
And they looked like new creatures
that just popped out of Zeus's head
and cannot be tamed, so they go on
whispering about the wind,
the sleet, the snow.

There Is an Expanding Crack

in my lower right wisdom tooth.
It's been itching and teasing me
for quite awhile now.
I go on, mostly oblivious,
walking my neighborhood, feeding the cat,
planting flowers in the ground.
The molar's days are numbered
and so are mine. But don't I possess
a decent smile, with almost straight teeth?
Isn't the light coming through
the eastern window today
just as vibrant as a painting by Cezanne?
I don't dwell on the knowledge of entropy,
or the fact of my short existence.
I spend down each day that comes along,
the dark ones and the bright,
rain or snow, hail or grief.

Three Billy Goats

Inside the tavern
of Three Billy Goats
I saw a figure in a corner.
Not just any ghost,
but the shroud of my father.
He sat at a dark table
with a flight of beers
on a small wooden tray.
His hair was combed neat,
his eyebrows trimmed
to stubby perfection.
I'd missed him on my walks
in the neighborhood, my swims
at the lake, the hapless
searches in hardware stores
for the right tool.
I had no one to argue
politics anymore, no doors
to slam over Vietnam,
or stairs to thunder up
over Watergate. I had to admit
from my own corner
of doubt and darkness,
how I longed to cross
the causeway between us.

Robin

Half way up
to the cardinals' nest
she sits in a clutch
of dreams.

A heated stillness
slows the wind.

Her circle of gathered
sticks and seeds
pockets the darkness.

The Song of the Common Sparrow

Inside the stiff branches
of an arborvitae
gray sparrows huddle and sing.
The snow falls steadily down,
bringing more cold and cruelty.
I stop to listen
as they rush through
the Hallelujah Chorus, the most
cheerful thing hidden in plain sight.
If I loiter here too long
they'll stop, go shy,
and flutter away.

Yesterday in Toledo

A steady downpour stained
an angel's silhouette
on the wall of the old cathedral.
Pigeons fluttered in the mud
beneath the faces of limestone martyrs

glaring down at our rumpled hearts.
We travelers filled the humid air
with the scent of exhaustion,
while the dark clouds of organ music
stopped us from walking any further.

And though I refuse to believe
in the resurrection of the body,
the Holy Ghost, or the communion
of saints, just outside

the church door,
I saw a man on a chipped
marble bench remove his
abrigo to cover two small boys,

letting the hard rain plaster
his own black hair to his head
in a kind of simple ritual
of ordinary redemption.

II

The Way We Argue

might someday win an award for endurance
and creativity. First, the pointed remarks
emerge and soar around the kitchen,
like a fly that got in through an open window.

Then, loud swearing begins that might awaken
Jesus, Mary, and Joseph from a comfortable sleep.

Who's turn is it anyway to do a few dishes
and take the garbage out?

A counselor once told us that arguing is good:
it displays significant markers of affection and trust.

But I'm not so sure. I think stuffing it down
may also demonstrate the fullness of love.

If we go to bed angry, it seems we both wake up
with rivulets of sorrow under our eyes,

where sleep lines and facial grooves
hold the dark words of the day.

Music Lessons

Before you came along and showed me
how to listen on the bed,
I had no idea of the form and tone
rising through the romance
of Schubert's songs, Beethoven's symphonies.
The world opened its little shutters for me,
and I saw gilded cities, shaped gardens,
the bright sky of a traveled world.
It's true, I taught you how to dance
and glide across the wooden floor,
as the orchestra floated its cellos and violins.
But you showed me how love
could add to the texture
of logic, melody, and sound.
I saw how you married a little chaos
to every morning's structure, waltzed
through it, your hands
moving just as quickly
as your mind.

Night Music

When I hear you snore
long past midnight, owls and crows
sing in my ear, I think of the sounds
of love-making,
and it comforts me to listen
to the push and pull of languid noises.
Starlight cannot be seen, and the man
in the moon closes his eyes.
A kind of lullaby takes over the room
and rocks my half-sleep
with a discordant symphony of subdued drums,
pale strings, a high flute rising
over the bass viol.
I love you most in the dark
when you can't see my face,
and your body tells me all the stories
I already know.

What Makes a Good Friend

for Marian

It isn't always obvious from the get-go.
Maybe we'll start with red wine
in a dark bar, sit together in near-silence
while making our plans
for walks and adventures.
The secrets she spills
I inhale, never repeat out loud.
She laughs at my jokes
and not at my attempts to be the clown
I strive to be. My feelings
are heard, not stuffed under a fancy hat.
She sees and understands the buttons
on my back, the one marked
poverty and shame, and the other
slow learner, and a third embossed
saved by the nuns of St. Vincent de Paul.
She never touches any of them.
I see her buttons too:
very shy and *adopted at birth.*
So here's to Cabernet Sauvignon,
and to us, and to the easy way
we've learned to bring ourselves
to the world.

She Knew How to Find It

That cat could stab the red ball from under the sofa
and cast the thing skittering over the floor

or dive for wads of paper and tossed notes
to chew the little clumps in wrinkles and wads

and swallow with pure relish any bit of wet pulp
to barf up later with pleasure and noise

or pull a ribbon of light from the top drawer
while you were in another room and oblivious

of the sunburst streaming in a dusty corner
and the slant of heaven holding her

The Last of the Sugar Maple

It looks good
from one side only,
like a middle-aged man
slowing in the alley
with the weight of sags
and lumps, handsome
around the darkened
hairpiece of leaves,
but from a distance
of five feet hurls
a whiskey scent
of insects and smoke
into the dead eyes
of its knobby features.
The knots and bellies
protrude out of proportion
to the height
of the promising limbs
wobbling in the wind.

Looking at Hats

I should have known there were others
crowding your mind
when I saw the parade of nubile women
wearing floppy hats on your computer.
Did you think I wouldn't notice
the polka-dots and madras plaids
dancing across your corneas?
I wanted so to be adored
in the early days, desired valentines,
chocolates, breakfast in bed.
I don't need all that anymore,
but I wish you would clear the screen,
get down to the business of paying attention
to the cirrus clouds sailing in
from the west, and the summer day
that billows ahead of us,
full of birdsong and clean air.

I Lost You in Edinburgh

where Cowgate Street meets Holyrood,
not too far from the Museum of Childhood.
You moved too fast through the dark
and brooding avenues.
Medieval faces in the cornices,
oval lights of alabaster, burned
right through me.
I looked for you in Fleshmarket Close,
and climbed the dingy stairs to an opening
of golden light, the color of whiskey.
I heard the faint summon of a whistle,
the fife and drum of the tourist trade.
I thought I glimpsed your bobbing head
in the crowd at Candlemaker Row,
a woman at your side.
When the rain returned in sheets
of blue, black clouds pierced
themselves on the spire
of St. Giles Cathedral.

I Saw You in the Lineup

hair greased back, black shirt and trousers.
I must say, you looked relaxed, loose
in the baggy clothes, at home and at ease.
Five faced forward, then turned
for the side shot, chins out, chests
puffed up and confident as grizzlies.
I'd pick you out anywhere:
snide, cocky, full of sins
you won't call sins, hurt
you won't call hurt.
All your smiles, teeth, swagger,
can't save you now, your flash
of silver, glint of gold.
Your metals don't add up,
only mirror the verisimilitude
of a full man.

He'll Come to the Door with Roses

Sometimes, I believe that a dead person
I used to know and desire
will visit me at my house, one
who I wanted, one who got away.
He'll come to the door with chocolates
in one hand, a bottle of Vintage Brut
in the other. Somehow I remember
he remembered me,
though the evidence looks sketchy
from the distance of years.
The nights he whispered his wishes
now seem a trick of lighting and shadow.
But he'll wear a gray suit, a black
handkerchief, appear sleek
and bold as a wolf.
I'll notice the faintest gray
in his temples,
as the moon fades before us,
and the stars remain unseen.

Iris Time

May's fleshy arrows
rise up in the border
between spring and summer.

Their colors tease our expectations,
unraveling surprises
in Prussian blue, royal white,
amber-yellow.

We bend and inhale
the new wines, the rich Bordeaux
of the dark one, or
the yellow-apple trimmings
of Pinot Grigio.

For two weeks we sip,
lean over, breathe in
the tart perfumes
of new light.

In the Dream You Lied to Me

right into the corner of my left eye.
I saw the monologue spin
like a pinwheel of shiny colors.
Spring had just opened
her curtains for us,
and the bark on the trees glistened.
After the cheat, your height shrank
a little, and your head slipped
down as if on a rusty hinge.
You held no pride
in your lying,
but couldn't stop.
I watched the sun shimmer
a false color in your runaway hair.
No one heard these words
except for me, the robins,
the worms.

Crows

Once, crows were my best friends.
I used to watch them strut beneath the pine trees,
showing their backside to each other.
No one seemed to notice that I was in their company.
Today I saw an old friend. Her black hair shimmered
like the sun-touched head of a god.
On seeing me, she turned her gaze away
to look into the green space just ahead.
My heart thumped, remembering a lie I told her
while urging thunder out of a silent sky.

Early March

A friendship slips
out of hand sometimes.
Perhaps the last
movie we saw together
ruined everything.
Comments I made
about the crude plot
may have wounded her.
Afterward, the beer
in the local bar
tasted bitter and flat.
I thought she had a cold
so I waited awhile,
and too soon
the emails stopped.
The weather shifted
from winter to spring.
Rain poured down
over snowbanks
and city icebergs,
unveiling bits of
candy wrappers and
broken wine bottles.
Not one, but two
Hawaiian leis
emerged in the cold
muck, and a purple glove
drifted along the curb
mismatched with
a red glove, fingers
curling upward.

Gluttony and Sloth

My companions
Gluttony and Sloth
travel where I go
around this room.
We watch public television
as the snow falls,
eat sharp cheddar
on rye, drink red
wine with chocolates.
On the evening news
wars continue,
women and children die.
The dishes are in
the sink now, so
we're almost ready
for the best time of all:
sleep. As we settle
down, we listen for
the two-toed creature
of stealth and violent
weather crawling
on the roof.

Ford Escort

Someone drove into our garden
late last night, and parked a rusty car
on top of white peonies in full bloom,
and crushed the stalks of Solomon's seal,
wheels deep in black dirt.
Who is she and why the act
of muddy vandalism?
The morning blew in cool, the birds
sang to each other in the maples
above her old car
abandoned on the flowers,
one wheel fender painted with possible
house paint, one tire a little flat.
Do you know her?
I thought I saw a flowered blouse
on the passenger seat, a small
purse near the brake pedal.
Why did she drive here
in the black of night
to trample over the best
of what we grew?

The Dream of Barbados

An elderly man from the hills
gave me gifts of oranges and limes.
His hands were the brilliance
of wet clay.
He asked me to help him down the slope
to the painted dock,
where people sail for the other world.
Wild dogs followed us,
sniffing at our heels.
Just before he stepped
into the tottering boat, seawater
spilled onto his shoes.
And for a moment,
the beauty of the waves
kept him from crossing over.

December

Sleep is the only way out.

In cruel wind I'm stiff-necked
and cold, losing luster.
I plunge into azure flannel sheets.

I see birds there, flashes
of color dance on the crests of trees.
Men wearing only shorts stroll in front of me.
Daffodils slumber
in their yellow sleeves.

I need sleep, yearn for a second pillow.
And when I'm very tired,
I can go great distances
in the right pair of pajamas.

Dream in Late January

We were visiting someplace warm
where birds chattered from telephone wires,
and a wind with a woman's perfume in it
brushed against the trees.
A sudden shadow dropped over us
the way a coin slips out of the pocket
and disappears with a shudder in the portico dust.
No one saw us there in the bright street,
happy and anonymous,
walking up and down the cobblestones
in search of people, excitement,
a place to drink wine.
Through open doors and windows
conversations drifted above the crowd.
We didn't want to talk at all,
nor did we understand the language.

Cinderella's Advice to the Stepsisters

If the slipper doesn't fit
don't worry, it's time to move on
to other shoes: mules, boots, or sandals.
Who knows, your best bet
might even show up like you,
barefoot and unhindered
and full of desire for sauntering
a sandy beach, ready for mulled
wine at a fire pit along the shore.
Don't be discouraged, darlings.
I kissed a lot of darkness
at the bottom of the hearth
before a princely one showed up
on his pale colt, wind in his hair.
Even then, I was distracted once or twice
by the shiny shoes of others.
Keep it simple, my dears,
it's not bloodletting, or the purge.
Let it all happen naturally, take
his hand and show him
how it's done.

The Kiss

Crimson trees line the street
like a row of women
with their hair on fire.

Red in the curtain folds
September light
all over the kitchen.

As the wind settles down,
burnt leaves rest
in pools of rust.

One airborne leaf
nicks the window
near my nose.

Bartender Monsieur Brown

In his most clever disguise,
I saw him give money to a stranger.
Other times he stood behind the bar
managing the cadences of space and time,
a conductor in a denim shirt.
He introduced his *mise en place*
relish or aperitif
woman to newcomer,
needing all of it in his tableau,
desiring applause, a big laugh.
I don't know why I loved him
after all this gray time.
Was it the undulating way he walked,
moving like a giraffe in the savannah
of a muffling corridor?
Or the way he eagerly sipped
seltzer from a plastic cup?
I'm still holding the zing in my mouth
for the green olive I stole from his little tray
when his back was turned.
I regret how sweet and salty,
I regret my teeth sinking in.
I regret the night I caught his eye,
and all the years I swallowed.

Snowman

I saw a man made of snow
and indifference
along my avenue.
He stood at mild attention
as the women walked by.
He had charcoal eyes,
and lips made of licorice.
Strong and tall,
he didn't seem to mind
the cruelty of the February wind.
And though I told my friends
I'm out shopping today,
I'm really inspecting other things:
muscles of sleet and ice,
shapes and strengths and opposites
of what I've known
so far.

Snowman II

My new snowman keeps a sunny face
in bitter wind and sleet.
He never lets his humble beginning
dishearten his outlook.

Hat, coat, carrot nose,
his eyebrows are cast from pebbles
found along the road.
I don't kiss him, but to wrap
my arms around him is pure fun.

How absurd to love his body
shaped by cold and vapor,
and rolled up tight
in the happenstance
of his own dirt.

Snowman III

Little man of frozen rain and swagger,
I think I recognize your mood today
under this full sun, loitering
here and looking for attention.
You seem to gaze just beyond me,
into the gray distance where birds fly.
Am I not enough for you,
do I not come by each day
and pack you back together,
round your head, smooth your belly?
When you start to shrink a little,
when your mittens begin to rot,
I might just let you go,
turn away from the shape
that once made me happy.
Your red scarf waves
in the bitter wind, almost
a daring gesture, but your arms
of sticks can't hold me.
Some dance partners can't be saved
once you see the sod underneath,
the jut of a chin beginning to fail.
What lies beneath anyway,
what heart of ice holds the black buttons?

Snowman IV

I tried to kiss you
in the open air, but the wind
brushed my face away.
I tried to reach inside your hat
to rub your temples,
but the sky turned from skim milk
to coffee gray and froze
my hands inside my gloves.
Someone left cigarette butts
next to the hollow
where your foot might be.
And now I detect drifting slush,
softness, a little mound of
middle-aged spread.
Are you letting yourself go?
I thought you might be here
for me longer than this.
But who am I to judge
and put a name on it,
aren't we all
just mostly water?

Snowman V

I saw you in the neighbor's yard today.
Your round face had become rounder.
You looked blindly past me
with your black bakelite eyes.

I recognized the green hat,
the Scottish scarf I loaned
you once, never desiring
to get it back.

Now you hide in winter drifts,
rooms of barren trees.
The sun licks against our bodies,
melting our days.
What shade of the blue sky
do you remember?

III

Innocence Lost

No chance he'll be back
in my corner any time soon
for a game of checkers
or the slow burn of pick-up-sticks.
No chance he'll follow me
like a brother, through a summer day
of sun and beach and dried grass,
the mower in the back yard broken,
the rabbit hutch empty.
He used to chase me like a freed animal
through a field of spider wort and ferns.
Now, the music on his car radio
plays the yearning songs
of girls and surfboards.
Squealing high out of the drive,
he's gone.

Some of My Friends on Facebook

have passed away, left the stratosphere
without a final comment or picture.
I sometimes sneak a peek at their pages,
longing to see their confident grins

and the beauty of what they knew,
the landscapes of river banks, the fields
of flowers at the bases of mountains,
the tricks of their talking cats.

I miss them, and I'm not that old
I tell myself, day after day,
counting the summers, the gardens
I planted, the friends I made

and lost, sometimes without knowing.
Where they went, I want to follow,
or at least to send a message,
a proud smile, a tiny heart.

What the Dead Remember

after Marvin Bell

They begin by remembering the scent of the human body,
the muted aromas of soaps and apples.
They long for the comfort of castaway things,
the towels and brushes, scarves and gloves.
They recall noise and clatter,
the danger of hidden knives.
They miss the cons and thefts, fondles
and empty kisses,
the abandoned beds of indifferent lovers.
They remember the coldness of cities,
the huddles of half-asleep workers,
silent sculpture.
They miss the window reflections, the mirrors
and bookshelves, the staring of eyes.
They remember the black and white flicker
of night traffic, family movies.
They miss the softness of human skin.

My Mother's Eyebrow Pencil

It rests on the lip of the sink.
Trimmed in red, with gold lettering,
I like the texture of the smooth wood,
the slender instrument in my fingers.

Crayon, chalk, cigarillo,
my mother smoked heavily,
even as she drew silhouettes and faces,
blending her paints with smoke.
A friend once said,
when the second parent goes
all strength lets loose
through the hands. Grit
earned the hard way
through work and love,
slips away.

I search the foggy mirror,
the outlines wither
behind steam and soap.
Traces of brow and mouth soften,
reveal cheekbones and teeth,
questioning the limits
of who we are.

The World Minus Joan

She disappeared in a yellowed robe
holding her make-up case, a cloud
of smoke collected in her eyes.

I looked up to see the clothing
piled up high on an emptied dresser,
the greens, browns, blues she wore.

I wanted go where she went, order
from the same menu.
I desired my black coffee
poured into a chipped cup,
craved the companionship of cold
blueberry pie.

I wanted to be with her then,
the learning done,
the work sharpened
on the oiled tool
of grief.

Remembering Diane

for MS Wachter

She used to collect me in her little blue Honda
almost every Sunday.
She'd never honk, but used the gleam of the sun
on the hood of her car to alert me.
We loved to get out of the city, head up
to North Branch, or west to Albertville
to shop for bras and shoes, hunt
for strong coffee, chocolate croissants.
Driving the freeway loosened something tight
in her, she loved soaring up the on-ramps,
negotiating her spot in the traffic.

On the way, I could say anything I wanted,
gossip about work, marriage, politics.
No judgment came from her,
no censorship or argument, no evading a subject.
But she knew the well-placed eye-roll,
the well-timed burst of laughter, how to give
a little advice without saying much.
She made me question my choices,
my crushes, my vote. I felt lucky
to have someone smarter around,
someone less experienced, but wiser.

Today, coming back to the city
from the northern suburb of Arden Hills,
the cirrus clouds raced and scattered
over the highway and towers of buildings,
and made me think of her,

of how we don't always notice the beauty
just here, the quiet and subtle
unfurling of light and color
rolling on right in front of us.

A Ray of Evening Dusk

for Eugene Trzebiatowski

When he went to help her in her old house,
he was told that the other guy helps more,
the other guy who looks just like him.

And being a strong son, he brought in a sack
of potatoes, but she really wanted flour and butter,
and the other guy brings chocolates, she claims.

She asked him to bring green grapes
but instead he brought red strawberries,
and already the dusk is the wrong color.

The other other guys comes early
and leaves late, and knows where the eggs
hide deep in the fridge.

And the other guys sounds just like him
but dusts under the table
and behind the stove.

When he looked into the kitchen mirror
he found his hair a mess, the part a zig-zag.
He looked like an animal coming out of hibernation.

In her living room, a slant of dark blue,
a ray of evening dusk
fell over the wooden furniture.

The other guy, she says,
kisses her on both cheeks
and tucks her in her little bed,

after pouring half a cup
of sweet cherry wine,
just to ease her longed-for sleep.

My Favorite Bartender

Wasting time on Facebook
the other day, I noticed
that another friend had died.
As a bartender, he had many fans,
a man about town, a handsome
devil, a midnight flirt.
He could be a snob, or sometimes
give you the shirt off his back.
I trusted him to do the right thing
for the occasion. There was a sense
of democracy about the man
who could talk to anyone, and did.
He looked into the hearts of people,
not with a glance or chitchat,
but by asking difficult questions,
even tossing a little Aristotle
or Epictetus their way,
just to see what they did with it,
to see how long they turned and twisted,
dousing or mulling the thought
from their bar stools.

Someone Very Tall

seems to follow me
down the icy sidewalk,
mumbling nonstop.

He shadows me
late at night,
a sudden darkness
in the singles' bar.

At the grocery store
he elbows me rudely,
as I study
a jar of pickled herring
resting in wine sauce.

Sometimes he trails me
all the way home,
twists my shame
in the driveway.

Then the moon displays
his lumpy face,
a lost lover
now gone.

September Evening with an Old Album

(listening to the Stones' Out of Our Heads)

A black and empty house is a curse
to those who love light
and need to bring in color
to worn and jaded pieces of furniture,

those dusty companions
loitering in the corners of a Saturday night.
I imagine landlords of the past
listening from the jalopy window frame.

An old album,
purchased with babysitting money in 1969,
waves in warps on the turntable.
Its sound absorbs the dull air:
heartbeat bass, rhythm guitar, a man's voice
like a trumpet over rolling drums.

I listen, amazed
at the boldness of desire
held so long
in a cardboard cover.

The Music of Other Stereos

That boy I think of from college,
tall and lean with long brown hair,
I'm glad we didn't take it to the limit
because all I recall now is one lukewarm kiss
after the final night of Introduction to Chaucer.
And that was it, I did not let him follow
me down the woolly path of youth
to the women's dorm, roommate gone,
monitor out on an errand, wing empty of spies.
It was my secret wish all along,
after I heard the praise from one friend
after another about the light touch
of his voice, the steady glow in his eyes.
But I believe I'm mostly happy
we didn't pulled out all the stops
in front of a poster of Jerry Garcia,
while the music of other stereos,
Dylan and Donovan, Carole King,
blasted along in near-harmony.

I've Come to Observe

from my lookout here in the neighborhood,
my cement stoop, dusty window,
that I haven't found the answers.
I have not met the gods and goddesses,
or the Green Man, the protector of soil.
Even here, truth and beauty
elude me, escape my hands.
The deeper I dig, the more rocks
I find in the dirt. The more weeds
I pull, I find poisonous ones,
many that I used to think were flowers.
I've become unsure about love, death, beauty.
With you, beneath a whisper of clouds,
I've learned to find a little peace
watching the birds in the cherry tree,
the simple way they sit up high
all day, out of reach.

Jackie in Her Garden

for Jackie Janson

She leads me in, while making the rounds,
picking up sticks and pine cones. She's Eve
in sneakers, moving color and shape.

A black branch outlines a serpentine
outlay of plants, many bursting new leaves.

Colors are arranged for surprise:
pale stripes next to emerald greens,
blues in the company of near whites.

I've never entered a painting before,
so I'm not sure where to place my feet.

We turn the corner, and we're far from done.
Who knew hosta came in thirty-two flavors?

Hydrangeas along her green and white house
pop their glossy fists.

She shows me the silk faces of Asian lilies,
the bearded astilbes, introduces a tiger lily
with beady black eyes, standing in full
glade, tall as Adam.

Child Labor

He's no older than five,
so the silence between himself and the world
keeps his head down.
He toils on cobbled streets in dry Mexico.
Good at moving weight, he balances
childhood and necessity,
and avoids the camera's eye.
The fine dust of road brick
lives on his hands, hair, clothing.
By the size of the haul, we see
he's done this before, lifts water and cement,
and knows how to lace the road with sweat.
He twists his small body into work.
His T-shirt says something unreadable:
American Rumor, or American Roommate,
or American Splendor.

A Winter Memory

Once, my father pushed open
the living room closet door
to check the line-up of winter coats.
The crumpled ones carelessly left
on floor or shelf
were tossed out the front door,
and onto the highest snow mountain.
Under the cold breath of January,
my hapless sisters and brothers scrambled
to recover their dignity and warmth
on the muted ride to school.

I'm Now Somewhat Afraid

of someone I love, some who comes to stay with me.
I'm fearful of her judgments and stares,
the casual way she casts aspersions on my dishes.
Once or twice I came up short,
didn't tip well, left a noisy party early.
And now she doesn't trust me
to do the right thing, give a juicy compliment,
bring a wrapped gift for the host.
My manners are not impeccable.
My clothes are never ironed.
It's true, I stand a little off center of others,
and in the solace of my own corner,
sometimes imitating a coat rack.
I'm with my loved paperbacks, my collection
of pristine vinyl records,
or holding up the northern wall of a room,
while taking comfort in whatever cat
or dog that happens to lumber by.

Padre

In the days since you've gone,
long ago and far away,
deep and dark and gone,
I don't worry anymore
about your judgments and tastes,
your grilled steaks and French wines,
your perfectly tuned car.
I no longer doubt
my own hair style and make-up,
the color of my shoes.
I spend nights with friends, cats,
dogs, the garden light
slicing the sorrows of the day.
I walk the city and up the hill
past the graveyard of need,
beyond the parking lot of want.
Some days are easier without your love
and its storyboard and map,
compass and slide-rule,
shaker and shot glass,
and all the other heedless ways
we measured beauty.

Evensong

When the evening folds into black,
trees hide in shifting clouds.

We sit among candles and lamps
in the cove of the back porch.

The music of the insects begins, dragons
and moths ping against the screen,

an introductory requiem
for those we have lost.

When the moon reveals herself,
our bodies almost disappear.

The call and response of the crickets' song
brings the darkness closer.

To the Last Warm Day

The last warm day, mid-September,
and the light spins through the trees,
ripples over houses.
What a season it's been, blue
and tangerine around the edges of evening.
The beaches we hounded
held sand so hot we had to run to the water.
At night, the aria of rain
spilled torrents on brick ledges,
cars, sidewalks,
pooling little lakes on the grass.
We'll remember the world in color,
emerald of oak leaves
shining straight to the eye.
Our rooms will grow cooler soon,
lonelier, darker.

Perusing the Book of Love

As the years fly by
I like to think that romance
will still grab us
once in a while.
I might discover you
perched like a scholar in a chair
reviewing
the instruction manual.
Perhaps the drawings
interest you most,
and you have forgotten
some of the lexicon.
If you memorize
the table of contents,
I'll take you out for dinner,
order your favorite bottle
of Vinho Verde.
I won't mind if you spill
a little, put your elbow in it.
The aroma will be
crisp and warm,
firm, but
not too dry.

Dragonflies

If we could glide
the way they do
over emerald waters
beyond the pungent
stalks of cattails
stuck together in sex
and flying at the same time
lock and key
just the blue sky
as an entry of flight
we would sail like fairies
with wings of stained glass
our shiny bodies
of burgundy and green
trembling
like falling leaves
in the pleasures
of sustained joy

The Elm Tree

I'd like to be an ancient one
someday, like this tree
lounging in front of us
with heavy arms,
stout trunk, an overcoat
of wrinkled bark.
I'd like to be both hard
and soft to the touch,
unembarrassed by knots,
healed scars, or hairy fissures.
I'd hold almost still
in the music, shivering
slightly in rain or thunder,
but alive in the rough blow
of changeable winds,
making shade for everyone
while bringing in
the darkness.

A Man Took His Cell Phone for a Walk

down Rollings Avenue.
A dog on a leash
pulled him steadily ahead.
I saw them slip into the shade
of an elm's new leaves.
Shaking his head,
the man peered into the small
screen, searching for something.
Cherry trees burst out in skirts
of pink and white ease,
and tulips lay low,
their red mouths tasting
the morning sun.
Nose first, the dog
sank into a hollow of grass,
as if the laws of patience
were a kind of sorrow.

Early Monday

Late for work,
I watch my bus crawl forward in the snow.
White flakes slowly bury a white car.
Overhead, an airplane sears the sky
while chimneys huff in pain.
New sunlight trembles against the houses
on Como Avenue, making each
south-facing window pane
a Russian icon
of lit gold.

Elegy for Bill Johnston

I thought I saw him yesterday
in the downtown library,
stepping from neurology
to quantum physics,
his large hand riding
the call numbers, codes
from another world.

He wore the same gray suit,
wild stripes underneath, opened
at the neck. His mustache twitched
as he moved from book to book,
glad-handing old friends.

The patrons seemed stunned
to see him there, the janitor
stopped dancing with her broom.

He retired early, unwound
his fishing line, carried out tackle,
reel and bait, to one green river
after another, taking on

steadfast shores of hidden stumps
to chase perch in low light,
full sun, shoal or wave,
never wasting a single hour.

August Field

Pig weed trails the greased ties
of the local railroad line.

An abandoned garden dries
our lungs with oregano and mint.

One yellow poplar leaf stuns us
with its early demise.
.

Inside a broken fence, peaks
of poison ivy ripen and turn,

while sparrows in the dirt
harvest the fading grass.

Counting the Years

Inside an attic's peak,
we look over furniture, radios,
blemished photographs.

Merging with each
other's shadows,
we touch and turn

porcelain dishes, pots
and pans, silver
wrapped in velvet cloth.

The remaining Sunday
half-light trembles
through wooden slats.

Cracked boxes
stacked two feet high
reveal vinyl records.

As we flip thru the dust
jackets, music
comes out of our hands.

Volunteer

Little plant with large tropical leaves
what are you doing here among the wild violets
and the jack-in-the-pulpits?
You should be in a swamp in Boca Raton,
or further afield in a jungle in Borneo,
learning to grow up near fishermen
as they catch the wilds of the day.
I hope you can make it to September
without being mowed down
or cut by someone's blunt scissors.
You look silly standing tall
between the common bungalows,
out of place as everyone
in this Como Avenue neighborhood, random
factory workers, students,
the fresh batch of assistant professors.
Transplants live here
at the industrial edge of the city,
people from Duluth, Fargo, Wisconsin
small towns, learning to work
and survive, not quite fitting in,
but hiding between grandma's peonies
and the latest variegated tulips
from Home Depot.

This Kind of Humble Day

As clouds drift toward us
and the last of the rain trembles
on the grass, I wonder
how long we can stay together.
Blue house, orange cat, rich
in lazy afternoons, we loll
barefoot on the back porch.
The wine goes down
like gold in our throats.
It's so easy here, the wind
bending the summer screens,
trees almost asleep
in their gray coats.
I hope we can take it all
the way, luck out here
among the rose bushes,
the pachysandra,
the darkening ferns.

The Dream of Thieves

Robbers broke down the back door
last night as we tried to sleep.
We could hear the laughter,
the shouts and boasts from our bed.

In the dark, they took it all:
the prints of Cezanne, Picasso, Canaletto.
The humbly framed things we loved
vanished from our house.

In the morning we saw
squares of furry dirt
on the walls, little shapes
of tombstones
stared back at us.

The Wild Dogs of Mexico

They hide under ramshackle tables
in fields and in gardens of shade.
I see their tough faces under flowering trees.

These rolling warts and patches
guard their strength,
while rummaging the dusty streets.
Some empty days they wander unlucky.

They never follow close, or look me in the eye,
but hold their heads down, keep low
like thieves stalking treasure,
letting shadows merge with shaded buildings.

Only at the ocean are they tame.
Their open mouths snap at the crests
of foam. They chase endless
waves, submerge themselves a little
to give away dirt and grief
at the playground of the sea.

The Garden Inside

I welcome the new wind
sweeping in from dark Montana.
At September's burnt end
breezes blow hot, then cool, menopausal.
The flowers I grew, I'll keep,
white geraniums for the southern window,
variegated hoya for the sleepy east.
I'll memorize the rest: tangerine tiger lilies,
lemon aster, the punk reds of bee balm.
I need them all against the weight
and depth of winter, the chilled rooms,
cold feet, bare maple floors.
From my stuffed chair, I'll gaze upward
to these colors in a love-lit trance,
and no one will wake me
or claim the summer dazzle
I steal to stay warm.

The Song of the Owls

In the landscape between people
and other wild animals

I've yet to find the boundary
between humans and birds

especially since I awoke to a flutter
in my black sleep last night

as wind and snow raced through the trees
and the last of the sleet churned softly

like a stranger touching the doorknob outside
with a muted tremor in the dark

I heard the tender bells in two-part harmony
of owls calling back and forth

as a pulsing search for light
from the darkness of midnight pines

About the Author

Carol Rucks graduated from the University of Wisconsin, Stevens Point, where she studied Literature and Creative Writing with David Steingass and Dave Engel. She also studied with Jude Nutter and Thomas Smith at the Loft Literary Center, and with Roseann Lloyd in Latin American as part of Art Workshops in Guatemala. She has worked mainly in libraries, especially the Art/Music/Literature reference desk at the Minneapolis Central Library.

Her poems have been published in *Abraxas, West Branch, Colere, Earth's Daughters, Poetry Quarterly,* and elsewhere. She is the author of the poetry collections *Evidence of Rain* (Nodin Press, 2014) and *Wavelength* (Kelsay Books, 2023). She lives in Minneapolis with her husband Mark McHugh.